RADIO

OTHER BOOKS
BY ALDEN R. CARTER

Nonfiction

Supercomputers
(with Wayne J. LeBlanc)
Modern China
Modern Electronics
(with Wayne J. LeBlanc)

Fiction

Growing Season
Wart, Son of Toad

A FIRST BOOK

RADIO

FROM MARCONI TO THE SPACE AGE
ALDEN R. CARTER

FRANKLIN WATTS
NEW YORK • LONDON • TORONTO
SYDNEY • 1987

Diagrams by Vantage Art, Inc.

Photographs courtesy of:
The Bettmann Archive: pp. 11, 19, 22,
24, 31, 40, 49, 50 (bottom), 53, 63;
Broadcast Pioneers Library:
pp. 17, 43, 50 (top), 54, 55;
AT&T Bell Laboratories: p. 70;
General Electric: p. 73; WNYC: pp. 74, 90;
Sony Corporation: pp. 77, 83;
NASA: p. 81; AT&T: p. 85.

Library of Congress Cataloging
in Publication Data

Carter, Alden R.
Radio: from Marconi to the space age.

(A First book)
Bibliography: p.
Includes index.
Summary: A history of radio from the
earliest experiments and discoveries
in wireless communicaiton to the
modern day communications satellites,
microchips, and cellular radios.
1. Radio—History—Juvenile literature.
[1. Radio—HIstory] I. Title.
TK6550.7.C37 1987 621.3841'09 86-23335
ISBN 0-531-10310-2

CONTENTS

Many thanks to all who helped with *Radio*, particularly my wife, Carol, and my friends Don Beyer, Jim Peterson, Dean Markwardt, Dick Sigl, Wayne Lauterbach, Sue Babcock, and Georgette Frazer. I owe special thanks to my technical consultants Dennis Suckow and Wayne LeBlanc.

For my friend and agent,
Ray Puechner

CHAPTER

I

A TRANSATLANTIC GAMBLE

The kite rose, plunged, then steadied against the gray sky over the Atlantic coast of Newfoundland. Standing below in the cold rain and wind, several men watched anxiously. The kite held aloft 400 feet (120 meters, or m) of antenna wire and the dreams of the young man who sat calmly drinking cocoa in the nearby cottage.

The date was December 12, 1901. The young man, who glanced at the clock, then set down his cup, was Guglielmo Marconi. The prearranged time had come. He walked to a table covered with equipment, accepted an earphone from an assistant, and began listening. On the southern coast of England, 2,000 miles (3,300 kilometers, or km) of icy ocean away, more of his assistants began sending a simple message to him. Over and over again, three short pulses of power leaped from their tower. In code the tightly spaced "dits" stood for the letter S.

George Kemp, who had handed him the earphone, watched Marconi's face anxiously. He knew that the inventor had bet both fortune and reputation on this attempt to send a radio message across the ocean.

At twenty-seven, Marconi was already a famous man. Only five years before, he had convinced the British post office to fund his wireless system to send messages through the air rather than along miles of telegraph poles and wire. The success of the Marconi system had been remarkable. Soon wireless messages were flying all over Europe. At sea, dozens of ships carried Marconi wireless. Kings, queens, and presidents marveled at the modern miracle and sought to meet the inventor.

Yet, this quiet, modest, handsome man was not without his enemies. Jealous scientists pointed to the young Italian's lack of scientific training. Telegraph and transoceanic cable owners fought to protect their profitable systems. Engineers in America and Europe rushed their own wireless systems into operation. If Marconi's latest experiment failed, his enemies might destroy him.

Most of the era's scientists would have laughed had they known of Marconi's ambitious plan. Almost all scientists agreed that radio waves traveled in straight lines, making over-the-horizon reception impossible. The waves, instead of following the curve of the earth, would continue on into space to be lost forever. Marconi intended to prove the scientists wrong.

None of the tension of the great gamble showed in his face as he listened for the signal on this early December afternoon. For several long moments he seemed to be listening with greater concentration. Then he calmly handed the earphone to Kemp. "Can you hear anything, Mr. Kemp?"

Kemp listened and heard three distinct clicks. They came again: the letter S. The radio waves from England had not shot off into limitless space but had somehow crossed the Atlantic to reach Newfoundland. Marconi and Kemp knew the significance of this moment: the era of worldwide radio communications had begun. Yet, they took only a moment to congratulate each other, then returned to the experiment, waiting once more for the dit-dit-dit to cross the ocean.

Guglielmo Marconi (1874-1937), photographed shortly before his momentous transoceanic radio transmission in 1901

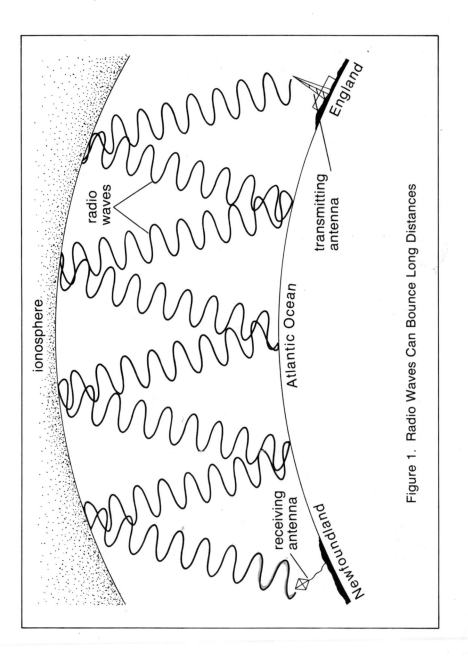

Figure 1. Radio Waves Can Bounce Long Distances

ionosphere

radio waves

England

transmitting antenna

Atlantic Ocean

receiving antenna

Newfoundland

Like many scientists and engineers before him, Marconi had proved that something would happen without knowing why. No one in 1901 knew that high above the earth there are belts of charged particles—called ions—that reflect some radio waves. The radio waves sent from England had crossed the Atlantic in a series of "skips," bouncing back and forth between the earth and the ion belts (Figure 1).

The ion belts form the ionosphere 50 to 400 miles (80 to 640 km) above the earth. Reflected waves return to earth in a shower, making it possible to receive radio messages over a wide area. Since the signal loses power in the process, it becomes fainter over distance. The time of day and season of the year alter the reflecting qualities of the ionosphere, further complicating long-range radio communication.

Within a year after Marconi's experiment, scientists seeking to find the reasons for its success discovered the first of the ion belts. Armed with this new information, Marconi and other engineers set about building a radio communications system for the twentieth century.

2

MYSTERIOUS WAVES AND FIELDS

Marconi was far from the first to imagine the possibility of wireless communications. Many scientists had been studying radio waves for years. In 1832, the great English scientist Michael Faraday had predicted their existence. The Scottish genius James Clerk Maxwell had proved Faraday's prediction mathematically in 1864.

Radio waves are one form of what are called electromagnetic waves. Radio waves, ultraviolet radiation, and visible light are all electromagnetic waves. They are called electromagnetic because the waves are produced by the two fields—electrical and magnetic—created by an alternating current of electricity. When a flow of electricity changes directions (alternates), waves of power shoot out in all directions at the speed of light, 186,000 miles (300,000 km) per second. Electromagnetic waves travel in what are called sine waves (Figure 2).

HERTZ'S EXPERIMENT

Although Maxwell's mathematical model was convincing, no one successfully produced and studied electromagnetic waves for

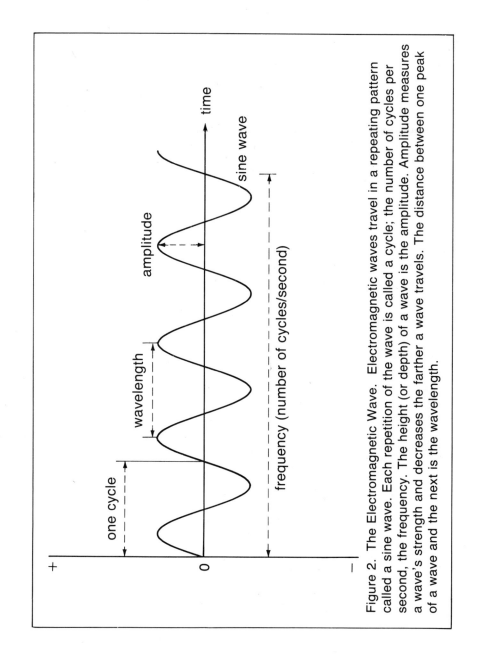

Figure 2. The Electromagnetic Wave. Electromagnetic waves travel in a repeating pattern called a sine wave. Each repetition of the wave is called a cycle; the number of cycles per second, the frequency. The height (or depth) of a wave is the amplitude. Amplitude measures a wave's strength and decreases the farther a wave travels. The distance between one peak of a wave and the next is the wavelength.

over twenty years. In 1887 a young German scientist, Heinrich Hertz, performed a series of experiments proving that electromagnetic waves existed outside Maxwell's calculations.

Hertz's equipment was simple (Figure 3). His device for generating electromagnetic waves had a loop of wire with two metal balls, one on each side of a narrow gap. The loop was connected to a coil of wire, a battery, a switch, and a device for storing electricity called a Leyden jar. When the switch was thrown, direct current (electricity flowing in one direction) from the battery was changed to alternating current (electricity reversing directions rapidly) by the coil and the Leyden jar. One ball of the loop gained a positive charge, the other a negative charge. As Hertz expected, a spark then jumped the gap from the negative to the positive side, neutralizing the charges.

When the alternating current reversed direction, the charges on the balls reversed, and a spark leaped the gap in the opposite direction. The process continued as long as the alternating current was supplied to the loop. Hertz named his device the oscillator, because the sparks were constantly jumping back and forth, or oscillating.

Next Hertz brought a similar loop of wire near the first. A small spark was also jumping across the gap between the two balls in this loop, even though no battery was attached! The alternating current in the transmitting loop was generating electromagnetic waves that crossed the distance to charge the receiving loop and produce oscillating sparks.

Further experiments proved that the waves traveled at the speed of light and, unlike sound waves, did not need air or water to conduct them. At some wavelengths, they could even penetrate solid objects.

Hertz's brilliant experiments sparked international interest, and scientists in many countries began studying the mysterious waves. A few began experimenting with them for communication. By turning a transmitter on and off according to a code, electromagnetic waves could carry a message to a receiver.

James Clerk Maxwell (1937-1879), the Scottish scientist who mathematically proved the existence of electromagnetic waves

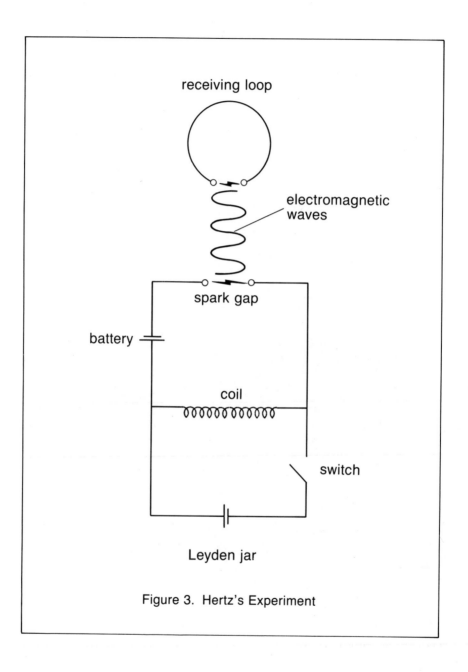

Figure 3. Hertz's Experiment

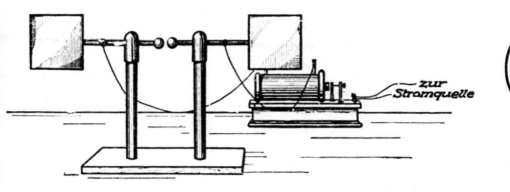

*An old diagram of Heinrich Hertz's early
transmitter for generating electromagnetic waves*

MORSE CODE

The simplest problem for the early radio scientists was choosing
a code. Since the 1840s, messages had been sent through telegraph lines according to a system called Morse code. An operator at one end used a spring-loaded switch called a key to turn
the electricity entering the line on and off rapidly. This produced a
series of quick bursts of electricity, separated by short periods of
no current flow and silence. Each letter of the alphabet was represented by a pattern of one or more short (•) or long (−) bursts
of electricity. (Sometimes the bursts of electricity were all the
same length, and the length of the silences between varied to
produce the Morse code letters.) For example: − −(M) •−(A)
•−•(R) −•−•(C)− − −(0) −•(N) • •(I). At the other end of the telegraph wire, another operator listened to the "dits and dahs" and
copied down the message.

EARLY TRANSMITTERS
AND RECEIVERS

Hertz's transmitter was a laboratory tool with low power. Transmitters had to be improved to send signals over longer distances. The early researchers built larger versions of Hertz's oscillator, calling these transmitters spark-gap generators.

The receiver Hertz used was impractical beyond a short distance, because the sparks created by the incoming waves were difficult to detect. Working independently, Edouard Branly in France and Oliver Lodge in England designed a better receiver. What was to become known as the Branly coherer was a glass tube filled with metal filings. When a radio wave struck the tube, the filings stuck together (cohered), allowing current from an attached battery to flow through the tube and ring a buzzer.

THE RADIO PIONEERS

By the mid-1890s so many scientists were trying to build practical wireless systems that the history of radio becomes confusing. No single person made all the important discoveries, and many discoveries were made at almost the same time by people working independently.

The early radio pioneers often worked in poverty, sacrificing nearly everything for their research. They took great financial and often physical risks to build their systems. The competition was hot. Jealousy, lawsuits, and treachery were commonplace. Even now, almost a century later, there is controversy about who invented radio.

The question may be impossible to resolve. However, an unknown young man with little formal education soon surpassed the others in designing and promoting a practical wireless system. In most history books, Guglielmo Marconi is called the father of radio.

3

MARCONI AND THE DEVELOPMENT OF RADIO

Guglielmo Marconi had been a quiet, solitary boy. He had few playmates on his father's estate in northern Italy. Yet, it was not an unpleasant life for a boy who loved to read and think. His Irish mother doted on him and shielded him from his stern father, who thought the boy a lazy daydreamer. Mrs. Marconi instructed her son in English, religion, and music. She also hired tutors occasionally, but Guglielmo preferred to pursue his own education.

His reading in the large family library led him to accounts of the work of Faraday and other great scientists. Marconi was fascinated by the mysterious force of electricity. He became an avid experimenter in his teens, working long hours in his attic laboratory. More often than not, his experiments ended in failure, but he would rethink his procedures, tinker with his gadgets, and try again. This determination and discipline led to discoveries that would make him a world hero long before his thirtieth birthday.

THE BIRTH OF A DREAM

The birth of the dream that changed Marconi's life and the world he lived in came on a summer day when he was on vacation in the

Marconi photographed in 1895 with his first transmitting device. He was only twenty-one years old at the time.

mountains. He was reading an obituary for Heinrich Hertz, whose short life had ended in January 1894. The article contained a summary of Hertz's experiments with electromagnetic waves. The idea of wireless communications came to the twenty-year-old Marconi in a flash.

The inspiration became an obsession. On his return to Villa Grifone, the family estate, he set about experimenting in earnest. He worked feverishly; the idea could not have escaped other men with more experience and better facilities. He had to catch up and surpass the others—and do so very quickly.

THE STRANGE MR. TESLA

Marconi was correct in thinking that others had similar ideas about wireless communications. The idea had already sprung from the mind of an eccentric genius named Nikola Tesla.

Tesla was born in 1856 in what is today Yugoslavia. He came to the United States as a young man and worked briefly for the great inventor Thomas Edison. They soon quarreled, and Tesla set up his own laboratory. In the 1880s, Tesla designed and built the first alternating current electrical system. It became the standard for the electrification of America, much to the disappointment of Edison, who favored direct current.

More than electrical generation interested Tesla. The range of his ideas was astonishing. He was interested in robots, submarines, lightning, death rays, and, of course, electromagnetic waves. According to the recollections of one of his assistants, Tesla demonstrated an experimental wireless in St. Louis in 1893, a year before Marconi read Hertz's obituary. The distance across the stage was only 30 feet (9 m), but the system was far superior to Hertz's oscillator and receiver. It had all the basic electrical and mechanical elements of the system Marconi had yet to develop. But Tesla's eccentricities and roving curiosity got the better of him. He went on to other projects, returning to radio later, but with impractical schemes that failed miserably.

Nikola Tesla, photographed
in his laboratory about 1910

The contrast between Tesla and Marconi was striking. Tesla was undoubtedly a genius, frequently working out complex theories in his head, but not taking the time to build the machinery to put them into practice. Marconi, on the other hand, was no theoretical genius, but a brilliant experimenter, fiddling with his machines until they performed a task he often understood imperfectly.

MARCONI BUILDS
HIS WIRELESS

In Italy, Marconi duplicated Hertz's experiments, then set about building a better system (Figure 4). He replaced the Leyden jar with a more durable device called a capacitor. On the suggestion of a neighbor, Professor Augusto Righi, Marconi installed a plate behind the spark gap to direct the waves toward the receiver. Most important, Marconi attached large copper plates to the sides of the spark gap. The plates served to store the electricity alternating in the circuit. When filled, they discharged, producing a larger spark in the gap and a more powerful transmission of electromagnetic waves. In the receiver, two similar plates were attached to the improved Branly coherer that detected incoming radio waves.

By the spring of 1895, Marconi was ready to bring his equipment out of the laboratory for testing. He was assisted by his older brother Alfonso, family servants, and a small group of friends that would expand as the years passed. Despite his solitary boyhood, Marconi was a natural leader. He demanded much, but was unfailingly polite and kind to his assistants. They responded with a fierce loyalty.

Marconi's signals were reaching out hundreds of yards by the summer of 1895. Yet progress was coming largely through increasing the power of the transmitter, and the inefficiency of brute force offended Marconi. A chance discovery produced a breakthrough. One day, Marconi laid one of the transmitter's

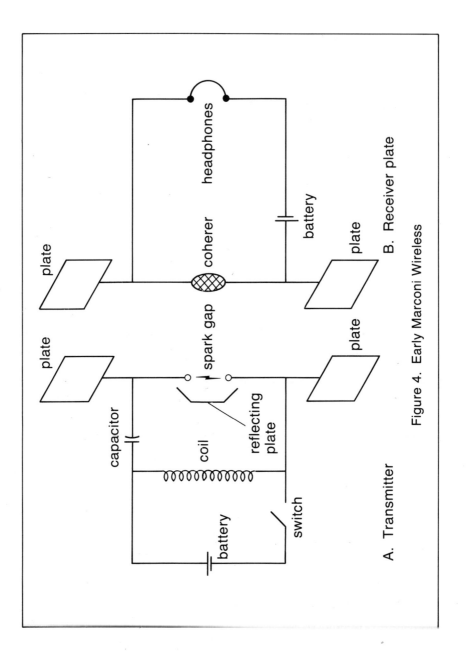

plate

plate

plate

plate

capacitor

coil

reflecting
plate

spark gap

coherer

headphones

battery

switch

battery

A. Transmitter

B. Receiver

Figure 4. Early Marconi Wireless

plates on the ground and held the other in the air. Immediately, the range of his signals multiplied.

Marconi had discovered the grounded antenna. Electricity was moving through the circuit into the ground, reducing the resistance to the flow of electricity in the circuit. The increased flow produced more powerful electromagnetic waves. Marconi soon found that he could get even better results by burying the ground plate and replacing the upper plate with a wire. Within a short time, Marconi was sending and receiving signals at nearly 2 miles (3 km).

It was time for a great test. He directed his brother Alfonso to take the receiver to the far side of a hill at the edge of the estate. Alfonso carried a rifle to signal if the signals were received. Marconi began sending and a shot rang out from beyond the hill. Marconi was elated; even hills and trees would not stop his radio waves.

SELLING WIRELESS

By early 1896, Marconi was ready to reveal his wireless system to the world. Even his father was now supportive. The patriotic Marconis offered the system to the Italian government but received a negative reply. Marconi was bitterly disappointed, but his mother told him not to despair and started contacting friends and relations in Ireland and England.

Mother and son were soon in London. Marconi set about repairing the equipment damaged by customs agents, who had insisted on taking many of the sensitive devices apart. He also applied for a patent on his system, convinced that other inventors would try to steal his valuable ideas.

He was ready to begin demonstrations in July. He carried an introduction to William Preece, engineer-in-chief of the British postal system. Preece was an elderly and prominent man. That he might have politely listened to the youthful Italian and then dismissed him would have been no surprise. Instead, Preece listened, watched a demonstration, and became Marconi's enthusiastic ally.

AMAZING THE WISE MEN

Preece arranged for some of England's most prominent scientists and engineers to witness Marconi's demonstrations. Some were skeptical at first, but not for long. Marconi kept increasing the distance of his signals. By the spring of 1897, he had achieved an 8½-mile (13.7-km) link across the Bristol Channel in southern England.

The commercial possibilities of wireless were quickly recognized. Marconi received offers to buy his system, but he refused to sell. Instead, he formed his own company, selling shares to investors but keeping majority control. At twenty-three, Marconi was proving to be an astute businessman. The Marconi Wireless Company would make him a wealthy man.

The new financial backing allowed Marconi to improve his system. He built larger transmitters and began experimenting with antennas hauled aloft by kites and balloons. On the southern coast of England, he built radio stations with tower antennas to warn ships approaching too close to dangerous waters. Marconi loved the sea and had always felt a bond with sailors. His shore stations and shipboard wireless installations were soon saving many lives. It was an achievement that he would take pride in all his life.

THE INTERFERENCE PROBLEM

Success brought new problems. Signals from the increasing number of wireless transmitters often interfered with each other, making good reception difficult. Marconi devised an improved system that allowed the tuning of his transmitters and receivers to specific frequencies (Figure 5). Tuning each transmitter to a different frequency greatly reduced the interference problems.

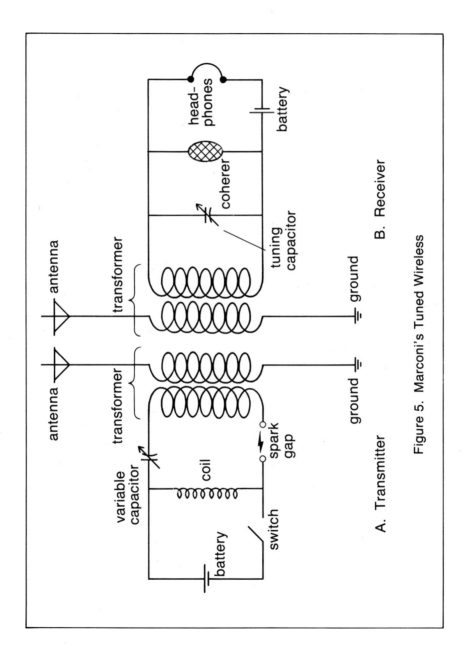

A. Transmitter   B. Receiver

Figure 5. Marconi's Tuned Wireless

Others, most notably Lodge, were also working to perfect tunable transmitters and receivers, but Marconi's system quickly became the most popular. His transmitter used a device called a variable capacitor to regulate the flow of electricity in the circuit and, hence, the frequency of the wave produced by the spark gap. In the receiver, a similar capacitor could be adjusted to select among the signals from different transmitters.

Marconi increased the efficiency of the transmitter by putting a transformer between the antenna and the oscillator circuit. (A transformer is little more than two coils of wire side by side. Without actually touching, the coils will transfer electricity from one side to the other.) The transformer improved the energy transfer from the oscillator circuit to the antenna, producing more powerful electromagnetic waves.

Marconi's improved receiver had a transformer between the antenna and coherer circuit. This design allowed the weak energy of the incoming signal to transfer more efficiently to the coherer circuit. The result was a receiver with increased sensitivity—the ability to receive distant signals clearly.

RINGING OUT
THE OLD CENTURY

Marconi was becoming a famous man. He had a flare for publicity. He sent wireless reports on a yacht race from a tug 35 miles (56 km) at sea. Tens of thousands of people read the reports in their newspapers—the first wireless messages most had ever seen. Soon afterward, the aged Queen Victoria invited Marconi to set up a wireless link between her residence on the Isle of Wight and the royal yacht. Marconi was delighted; the publicity would further his work.

In 1899, Marconi established a commercial wireless link across the English Channel, a distance of 32 miles (52 km). His first message read, "MARCONI SENDS HIS RESPECTFUL COMPLIMENTS ACROSS THE CHANNEL THIS FINE ACHIEVEMENT BEING PARTLY DUE TO THE

Marconi in Newfoundland in 1901 with the instrument with which he received the first transatlantic message

REMARKABLE RESEARCHES OF M. BRANLY.'' As always, Marconi was graciously paying tribute to the contributions of others in the development of wireless.

Still, wireless and Marconi himself were not universally popular. The companies that owned the underwater telegraph cables across the Channel resented the competition. Rivals such as Lodge and Tesla were challenging Marconi's patents. Marconi refused to bicker with rival interests in public. He knew, however, that he needed a stunning achievement to ensure the future of his wireless and his place in history. He was soon talking privately about "the great thing"—spanning the Atlantic with a wireless signal.

On that stormy December afternoon in 1901, Marconi would triumph. His achievement would open an era of spectacular advances in radio.

CHAPTER

GIVING RADIO
A VOICE

On Christmas Eve, 1906, operators on scores of ships off the east coast of the United States sat hunched over their wireless sets, waiting for the evening's message traffic. The professional operators were hardly the only ones listening on this evening. Wireless had caught the imagination of the age. In basements and attics ashore, hundreds of "ham" operators were fiddling with their amateur sets. For many unsuspecting professionals and amateurs alike, this would be an evening they would remember all their lives.

Wireless had come a long way in the few years since Marconi had first spanned the Atlantic. Most large ships and many smaller ones were outfitted with wireless. Ships and shore stations exchanged a flood of messages daily. These included weather reports, news updates, business and personal communications, and, every so often, pleas for help from ships that were in distress.

"CQ CQ"—the code for "All stations, I have messages for you"—leaped from the antenna of a small station at Brant Rock, Massachusetts. Dozens of operators heard it and leaned forward, ready to copy the dits and dahs. Many of them must have thought they'd lost their minds in the next few seconds; instead of the on and off pulses of Morse code, they heard a man's voice in their headphones, followed by a pause, then concluded by music.

Hams yelled for family members, shipboard operators for their officers. Those who rushed to listen confirmed that indeed music was coming from the headphones. The voice returned to read a Bible passage and then to invite all listeners to contact R. A. Fessenden at Brant Rock. Silence, the crackle of static, then operators all along the coast were calling one another in Morse code: "Did you hear it?"

At Brant Rock, Professor Reginald Aubrey Fessenden, a big bear of a man, savored his success. Fessenden was a Canadian-American scientist who had worked for years to make possible this stunning demonstration of voice broadcasting. The largest obstacle had been designing and building a transmitter to replace the spark-gap generator, whose oscillating sparks were too slow and unsteady for voice signals.

Dr. Ernest Alexanderson, a brilliant young engineer working for the General Electric company, built the transmitter Fessenden needed. Using the Alexanderson alternator, Fessenden produced his broadcast using a technique called amplitude modulation (Figure 6).

The alternator generated a steady signal—called a carrier—at a frequency of 50,000 Hertz (Hz, or cycles per second)—ten times the frequency produced by the highest-frequency spark-gap generator. A microphone converted the sound waves of Fessenden's voice and music into an electric current called the audio signal. The changing amplitude of audio signal carved (modulated) the peaks and valleys of the steady carrier, producing the wave broadcast from the antenna.

Fessenden's demonstration was a dramatic success, but many problems had to be solved before voice radio became a practical alternative to wireless.

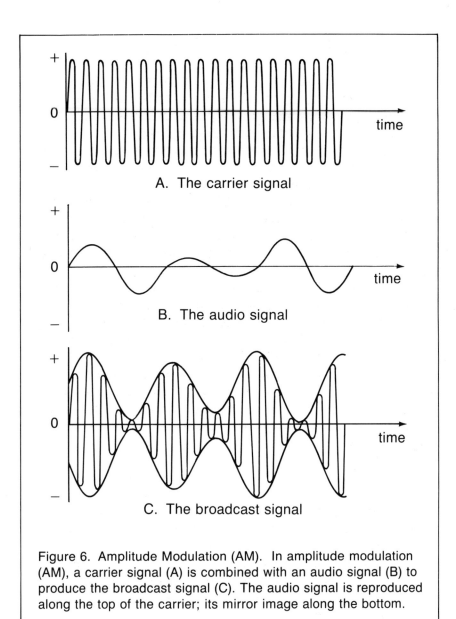

A. The carrier signal

B. The audio signal

C. The broadcast signal

Figure 6. Amplitude Modulation (AM). In amplitude modulation (AM), a carrier signal (A) is combined with an audio signal (B) to produce the broadcast signal (C). The audio signal is reproduced along the top of the carrier; its mirror image along the bottom.

THE SEARCH FOR BETTER RECEIVERS

The receivers of 1906 were designed to receive Morse code. Several ingenious designs had replaced earlier receivers based on the Branly coherer, but most Morse code receivers lost part of a complex voice signal or reproduced it poorly.

An exception was the recently introduced crystal receiver (Figure 7). The receiver utilized a mysterious characteristic of some crystals, minerals whose atoms are arranged in regular geometric patterns. Crystals could be used as detectors in receivers, changing the alternating current (AC) from an antenna to a direct current (DC). Adjusting the contact between a thin wire connected to the headphones and the surface of the crystal produced clear reception.

Crystal receivers worked well for voice reception, since a crystal detector and a capacitor could remove the carrier from an amplitude-modulated (AM) signal, leaving only the audio wave that had ridden the peaks of the carrier. This audio signal was converted back to sound by the headphones.

Cheap, reliable, and compact, crystal receivers became popular with hams and professionals alike. However, crystal sets had a major limitation: they worked on the tiny power of the received signal, and the output from the crystal could not be easily amplified, or increased.

THE EDISON EFFECT

The solution to the amplification problem lay in a nearly forgotten principle called the Edison effect (Figure 8). The great American inventor Thomas Edison had stumbled on the effect in 1883 while trying to improve his electric light bulb. The light-producing element of Edison's bulb was a carbon thread called a filament. When electricity passed through the filament, the filament glowed white hot, producing a bright light. However, the inside of the glass blackened with time, reducing the bulb's illumination. In an

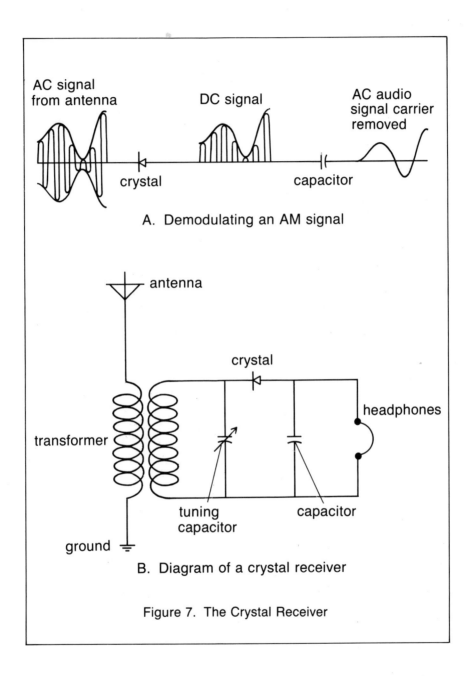

AC signal from antenna

DC signal

AC audio signal carrier removed

crystal

capacitor

A. Demodulating an AM signal

antenna

crystal

transformer

headphones

tuning capacitor

capacitor

ground

B. Diagram of a crystal receiver

Figure 7. The Crystal Receiver

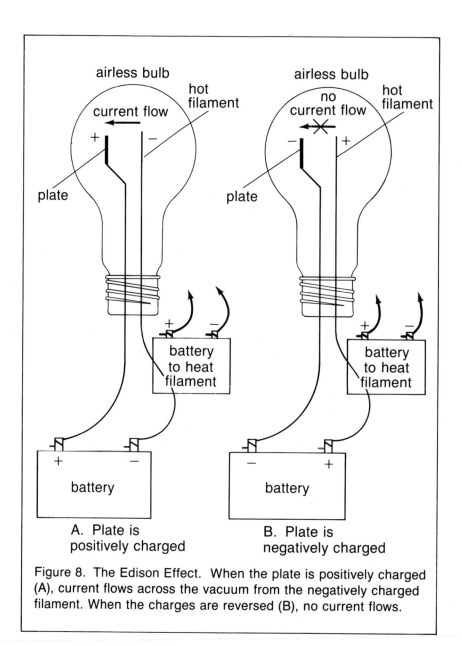

Figure 8. The Edison Effect. When the plate is positively charged
(A), current flows across the vacuum from the negatively charged
filament. When the charges are reversed (B), no current flows.

attempt to eliminate the blackening, Edison built a bulb with a small metal plate near the filament. He connected the positive (+) side of a battery to the plate and the negative (−) side to the filament. His idea was that the positively charged plate would attract the black particles.

Instead, something completely different happened: a current flowed from the filament to the plate. When he reversed the battery connections, no current flowed. Edison described this strange one-way-only flow in his journals, but since he saw no immediate use for the effect, he abandoned further investigation.

It is understandable that Edison failed to appreciate the potential value of his discovery. In 1883 no one understood that electricity was the flow of tiny negatively charged particles called electrons. The discovery of the electron in 1899 by the English scientist J.J. Thomson led to an explanation of the Edison effect. The hot filament of a light bulb emitted billions of electrons. Normally, this cloud of electrons hovered around the filament. However, when a positively charged plate was present, the electrons flowed toward it. If the charges on plate and filament were reversed, the electrons were repelled by the negatively charged plate and sucked back in by the positively charged filament. All electrical flow stopped abruptly, since the plate was not heated and emitted no electrons to flow toward the filament.

In 1904, John Fleming, an English electrical engineer, harnessed the Edison effect in the first of a new family of radio devices called vacuum tubes. Fleming named his invention the "valve," because it turned the flow of electricity on and off much like a valve in a water line. Engineers soon began calling it a diode, which means two electrodes (Figure 9).

Fleming replaced the metal plate used in Edison's device with a cylindrical metal sleeve around the filament. A battery heated the filament, but the plate was left cold. When an AC current was fed into the vacuum tube, electrons flowed easily from the filament to the positively charged plate for one-half of each cycle.

John Fleming, inventor of the vacuum tube

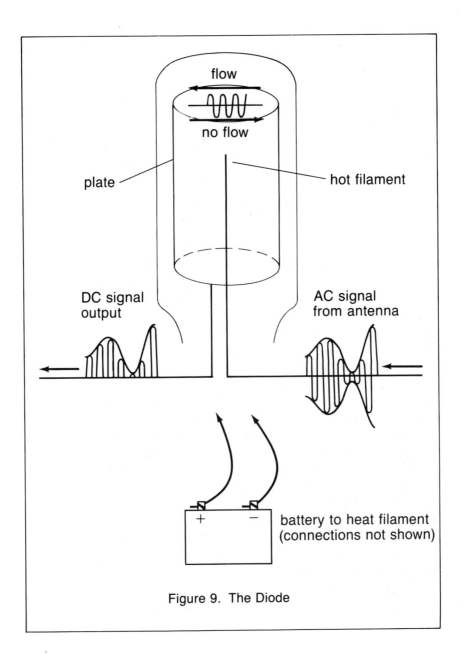

Figure 9. The Diode

However, when the current reversed, so did the charges on the plate and filament. The flow of electrons stopped as the negative charge on the plate repelled them and the positive charge on the filament pulled them back in. Fleming's diode changed AC to DC, serving the same purpose as a crystal in a radio receiver.

The diode was more flexible than crystals, coherers, or magnetic detectors. However, it was also bulky, fragile, and expensive. Another important step had to be taken before vacuum tubes could show their worth.

THE TRIODE

In 1906, an American inventor, Lee De Forest, modified Fleming's diode to create a device called a triode. De Forest placed a circular mesh of fine wire called a grid between the filament and the plate of a diode. Small changes in the negative voltage applied to the grid regulated the flow of electrons from the filament to the plate. Lowering the negative charge allowed more electrons to slip through the grid. Raising the negative charge decreased the flow because more electrons were repelled.

The triode was the first electronic amplifier. In combination with a capacitor, a triode could greatly increase the power of a weak audio signal. The filament and the plate of the triode were attached to the poles of a powerful battery, creating a strong flow of electricity from the filament, through the grid, to the plate. The grid was connected to a wire carrying the weak audio signal. The variations in this weak AC current varied the charge on the grid and, hence, the amount of DC current allowed to flow from filament to plate. The result was an exact but far more powerful copy of the audio signal. Several triodes could build a signal from a distant station to the point where it could be heard not only in headphones but in speakers.

Diodes and triodes gave engineers the tools to build better equipment for the transmission and reception of voice signals. Several years were needed to perfect the early vacuum tubes,

The first vacuum tube, photographed in 1904

but the development of practical voice radio was just around the corner.

PROGRESS ON MANY FRONTS

The years between 1906 and 1914 saw many developments in radio. Transmitters were built that soon dwarfed Alexanderson's 50,000-Hz alternator. New antenna systems were designed, vastly increasing the range of signals. Directional antennas were introduced to aim signals at a distant target rather than broadcasting in all directions. Radio signals—both Morse code and later voice—were sent to another new invention, the airplane.

A young graduate student at Columbia University in New York named Edwin Armstrong made two striking discoveries about triodes. In 1912, he found that a triode's amplifying power was increased if part of the output signal was fed back into the input side. Continuous reinforcement increased the amplification hundreds of times. His invention is called the regenerative, or feedback, circuit.

Armstrong's second discovery was equally important. He noticed that when the feedback reached a certain level, the triode not only amplified signals but also began to generate them. Hence, the triode could be used as an oscillator in transmitters.

The twin discoveries marked the start of a brilliant career for Armstrong. Many other gifted engineers were also working on radio in this period: Fessenden, De Forest, Fleming, Tesla, Alexanderson, and Lodge, to name but a few. Most either headed their own companies or were employed by large corporations. The time of the individual inventor working alone or with a small group of assistants was passing. Large companies with powerful laboratories were concentrating on the development of radio. The largest and most influential was the Marconi Company, and Guglielmo Marconi, still a young man in his late thirties, was still the most famous radio engineer in the world.

Marconi left voice transmission to others and concentrated on building a worldwide wireless system using Morse code. Marconi's research centered on sending radio signals reliably over greater and greater distances. In 1907 he established full-time radio service between Europe and America. Other intercontinental links soon followed.

THE *TITANIC*

The value of the Marconi wireless was brought home to many by a great disaster. Late in the evening of April 14, 1912, the largest and most luxurious ship ever built slammed into an iceberg in the North Atlantic. The engine rooms of the "unsinkable" *Titanic* were soon filling with water. The new distress signal—SOS—went out from the ship's radio mast. Less than 10 miles (16 km) away, the small liner *Californian* had stopped, surrounded by ice. She carried only one wireless operator, and he had gone off watch. Almost within sight of the sinking *Titanic,* the *Californian* did not respond to the SOS.

The *Titanic*'s lifeboats were launched, but there were far too few for all the passengers. The senior wireless officer, John Phillips, stayed at his post, tapping out the distress call over and over. Forty minutes after the accident, the liner *Carpathia* answered. Phillips gave the situation to the dumbfounded operator aboard the *Carpathia*: the unsinkable *Titanic* was going down. The *Carpathia* altered course and steamed at full speed through the night. At 1:20 A.M. the *Titanic*'s messages ceased; the *Titanic* had sunk. The *Carpathia* arrived on the scene at daybreak, too late for 1,513 of the 2,224 who had sailed on the maiden voyage of the mighty *Titanic*. John Phillips was among the drowned.

The news of the *Titanic* disaster was transmitted around the world by wireless. Marconi was in New York City and went aboard the *Carpathia* when it docked. He listened with tears in his eyes to the assistant wireless officer's account of Phillips's courageous final watch. When Marconi walked back down the gang-plank, the crowd on the pier cheered the man whose device had saved over 700 from the *Titanic.*

GOVERNMENT REGULATION

The sinking of the *Titanic* had a major impact on the development of radio. Wireless had saved lives, but the inadequacies of the system were glaringly obvious. The *Californian*'s operator had gone off watch, and hundreds had needlessly perished. Further inquiries revealed that the *Titanic* had either ignored or not received ice warnings.

Government regulation of radio had been lax or nonexistent before the tragedy. In its aftermath, new regulations were estab-lished and the development of the worldwide radio network became more orderly.

The increased interest of governments in radio came at a time when the world was sliding toward a disaster immeasurably greater than the sinking of the *Titanic.* In August 1914, World War I erupted in Europe. Radio would play a major part in the most terrible war humankind had ever known.

RADIO COMES
OF AGE

World War I (1914–1918) was the first war to see the widespread use of radio. Generals and admirals used it to control the distant movements of armies and fleets. Field commanders found it a valuable tool for coordinating attacks and defenses. Artillerymen could aim their guns with great accuracy using the spotting reports from airplanes equipped with wireless.

The use of radio opened a new field of spying. Listening to an opponent's transmissions could provide valuable information. Stealing or breaking codes became an important military concern. Even if messages could not be broken, the simple act of transmission could reveal information. The British pioneered radio direction finding, building stations to listen for the transmissions of German ships and submarines. If two or more stations picked up a signal, the position of the enemy could be calculated and British ships sent to the attack.

During the war years, engineers and scientists on both sides worked furiously to develop radio equipment and techniques. Governments forced a halt to cutthroat competition, and individuals and corporations cooperated in the war effort. By the time peace returned, radio equipment had been made more powerful, compact, and reliable.

One of the soldiers going home was pondering an extraordinary idea. While serving as a Signal Corps officer, Edwin Armstrong had conceived a voice receiver far better than any in existence: the superheterodyne. Armstrong returned to the laboratory to refine his idea and build a working model.

CORPORATE WARS

While Armstrong worked, several large corporations engaged in a battle for the future of the radio industry in the United States. The Radio Corporation of America (RCA), a subsidiary of General Electric (GE), opened the war in 1919 when it bought the American interests of the Marconi Company and exclusive rights to send wireless messages into the Marconi international network. RCA then formed an alliance with the giant telephone company American Telephone and Telegraph (AT&T), creating a virtual stranglehold on the American communications industry. The third major American radio company, Westinghouse Electric, was cut out of the deal.

The only field left open to Westinghouse was the sale of radio equipment to amateurs. Interest in ham radio was booming because of wartime developments in voice radio. No longer was the ham required to spend long hours learning and practicing Morse code. With a little ingenuity and a few dollars, the ham could build a voice receiver and a low-power transmitter.

Edwin Armstrong (1890-1954), inventor of the superheterodyne receiver and pioneer of FM radio, shown with his "portable" radio

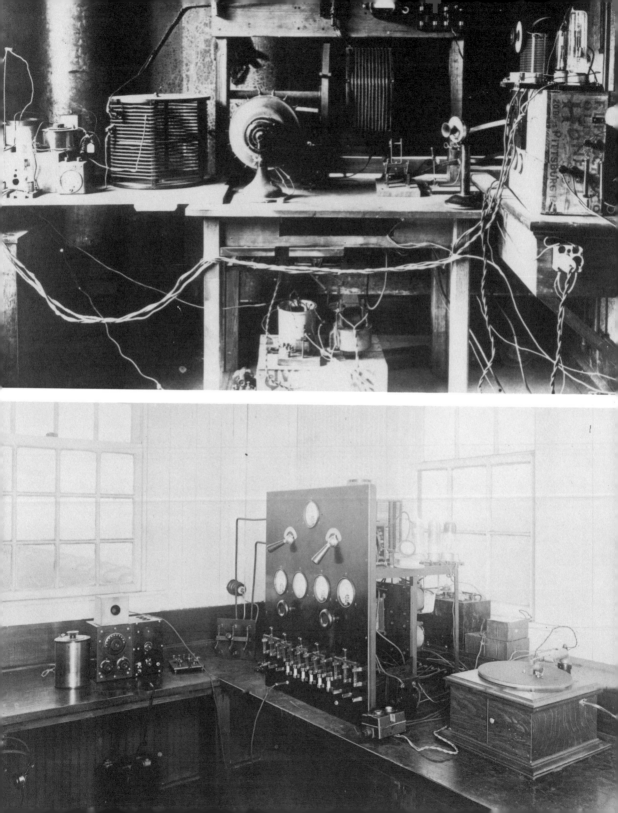

BROADCASTING FROM A GARAGE

Developing better equipment for the amateur market became the responsibility of a Westinghouse engineer, Dr. Frank Conrad. Conrad, a wiry man with a huge capacity for work, accepted the job on top of his already heavy responsibilities in Westinghouse's Pittsburgh laboratories. Much of his work on radio equipment was done on evenings and weekends in his garage workshop. Many hams in the area were happy to cooperate when he requested their help in testing an improvement.

To amuse his unseen assistants, Conrad began playing records. The hams responded enthusiastically. Soon Conrad was broadcasting for two hours, twice a week, occasionally including live musical performances by friends. News of the broadcasts spread quickly. A downtown store installed a radio receiver to attract customers and advertised radio sets—"ten dollars and up"—guaranteed to bring in "Dr. Conrad's popular broadcasts." Sales soared.

H. P. Davis, a Westinghouse vice-president, read the store's advertisement and wondered what full-time broadcasting might do for Westinghouse sales. He ordered Conrad to set up a radio station on the roof of a tall Westinghouse warehouse. On November 2, 1920, KDKA—the world's first commercial radio station— went on the air with a running tally of the returns in the Harding-Cox presidential election. The enthusiasm of the audience was beyond anyone's wildest expectations.

Above: *Equipment used by Dr. Frank Conrad, assistant chief engineer at Westinghouse, in the years before the first radio was established in 1920.* Below: *The original broadcast transmitter of KDKA, Pittsburgh, when it went on the air November 2, 1920*

In its first few months, KDKA broadcast live and recorded music, news, the first radio church service, political addresses, a fund raiser for refugee relief in Europe, a boxing match, agricultural market reports, baseball games, and a theater performance. Westinghouse was swamped with orders for its sets.

A REVOLUTION IN RADIO

The launching of KDKA began a revolution in the radio industry. It seems amazing now that the potential of commercial radio broadcasting had been ignored for so long. Fessenden and later De Forest had made widely publicized experimental broadcasts well before the war, and several experimental stations had broadcast on a more or less regular basis in later years. Yet, no major company had lent support.

Perhaps broadcasting's most persistent advocate was a young radio executive named David Sarnoff. He had tried repeatedly to sell his superiors at the Marconi Company and later RCA on the idea of a "radio music box" for the home. However, the senior executives had seen radio—like telegraph and telephone—as a method of two-way communication between private parties. The idea of broadcasting in one direction to listeners who paid nothing hardly seemed profitable. The huge success of Westinghouse's KDKA forced the RCA executives to recognize their error. Sarnoff was promoted, beginning a climb that would take him to the highest levels of the industry. Westinghouse was invited to join the GE/RCA/AT&T monopoly, and an uneasy truce was declared in the corporate wars.

"Radio frenzy" swept America. Eighteen months after KDKA's first broadcast, 220 radio stations were on the air and the number of radio sets in homes had jumped from 50,000 to somewhere between 600,000 and 1,000,000. Millions of Americans spent part of their evenings listening to "the magic box." Radio performers became overnight celebrities. Old and new

The KDKA studio in East Liberty, Pennsylvania,
from which a pioneer farm program was conducted

Above: *An early publicity photograph used to glamorize the use of radio receivers. The people in the picture are hooked up to an Aeriola Jr., the first popular-priced radio (it sold for $25).* Facing Page: *"Radiomania"*

RADIO NEWS

REG. U.S. PAT. OFF.

25 Cents
February
1924
Over 200 Illustrations

Edited by H. GERNSBACK

"CRACK IT WITH MUSIC!"

IN THIS ISSUE
THE ULTRADYNE
CIRCUIT
BY R. E. LACAULT
See Page
1058

THE 100% WIRELESS MAGAZINE

products became popular because listeners heard them advertised on radio.

OUT OF THE LABORATORY

The home radio receivers of the early 1920s were primitive. Large, ugly affairs, they were incapable of receiving distant stations most of the time. Operation was a chore, requiring the patient tuning and retuning of each amplifier stage. But Edwin Armstrong would soon change all that.

In 1923, Armstrong was ready to demonstrate his superheterodyne receiver. He arrived for a meeting with RCA executives carrying a "superhet" in his arms. It was tuned to an opera, the reception steady, clear, and loud. The executives gawked—where was the antenna? Armstrong explained that the set was so sensitive that it required only a small internal antenna. He put down the set and demonstrated how it could be tuned with little difficulty: the listener simply selected a station with one knob and set the volume with another. The executives immediately placed orders.

Armstrong's receiver gained quick acceptance by the public. By 1927, 7.5 million radio sets had been sold in the United States, the majority superheterodynes.

THE SUPERHETERODYNE SYSTEM

Almost all radio receivers down to the present have used the superheterodyne design. To heterodyne means to mix, or "beat," two signals of different frequencies. The superheterodyne receiver has an oscillator (a triode) which produces a signal to beat against a signal received by the antenna. Selecting different stations is accomplished by adjusting the tuning control to change the frequency of the oscillator. Whatever station is selected, the difference between its frequency and the oscillator's is always the same. This design makes it possible for the superheterodyne to detect a large number of frequencies, then select and amplify a frequency with ease.

Figure 10 shows a transmitter and superheterodyne receiver in simplified form. At a radio station, a microphone converts sound to an audio signal. A second signal, the carrier, is generated by a radio frequency oscillator set to the assigned frequency of the radio station. The two signals are combined in the modulator, amplified, and sent to the antenna. The movement of the combined signal in the antenna produces the electromagnetic wave sent into space.

On the receiver side, electromagnetic waves from many stations create electrical signals in the antenna. These signals are amplified and fed into the mixer where they are "beaten" with the signal from the local frequency oscillator. Different stations are selected by changing the frequency of the oscillator's signal. The selected signal from the mixer is sent through another amplifier to the demodulator (a diode, capacitor, and assisting components). The demodulator removes the carrier and sends the audio signal through another amplifier to the speaker, where the audio signal is converted back to sound.

RADIO BROADCASTING EVOLVES

Radio broadcasting expanded at a tremendous rate in the 1920s. In the first three years after KDKA began broadcasting, hundreds of companies established private stations to advertise their products. That year, AT&T's station WEAF in New York City began offering a cheaper alternative. WEAF announced it would sell air time to any advertiser interested. AT&T refused to share this immensely profitable idea with RCA and Westinghouse, invoking a clause in the original monopoly agreement to prevent the other companies from selling air time.

AT&T had another weapon in the renewed corporate wars: networking. Using its network of telephone lines, AT&T could send WEAF's programs all over the country for simultaneous

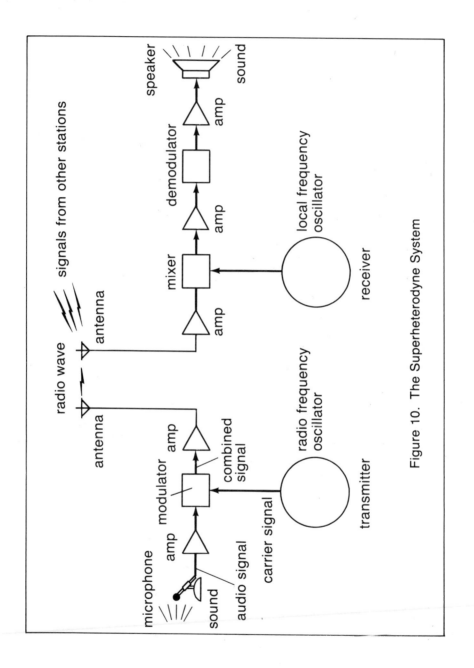

Figure 10. The Superheterodyne System

broadcast by other stations. Without open access to the nation's telephone system, the other monopoly members were thwarted from founding their own networks.

AT&T's effort to win complete control of broadcasting fell short. Government officials objected to the prospect of one company controlling both telephone and radio industries. Hundreds of independent stations casually ignored AT&T's legal rights by selling airtime and starting small networks. In 1926, the monopoly companies signed a new series of agreements profitable to all. AT&T retired from radio broadcasting. Its innovations—paid commercials and networking—remained to shape the future of broadcasting. In 1927, RCA established the National Broadcasting System (NBC). The Columbia Broadcasting System (CBS), a network of independent stations, soon followed.

THE NEED FOR REGULATION

By the mid-1920s, the radio industry had grown so large that overcrowding and abuse of the airwaves threatened chaos. Some 700 radio stations operated on the few frequencies the government had assigned for broadcasting. Reception was often horrendous as signals from different stations overlapped. Transmitter battles were waged in many cities as stations boosted their power far beyond legal limits to drown competitors' signals. Many stations changed frequency in defiance of regulations, and unlicensed operators further overloaded the airwaves.

Congress responded to the chaotic situation by establishing the Federal Radio Commission (FRC) in early 1927. Armed with a new set of laws, the FRC moved to restore order.

THE GREAT DEPRESSION

As the "Roaring Twenties" drew to a close, most Americans looked forward to another prosperous decade. However, disaster struck in 1929. The stock market "crashed," banks and businesses went broke by the thousand, and millions of people were thrown out of work. It was the beginning of ten years of hard times called the Great Depression.

At first it seemed that the radio industry would suffer like nearly every other industry, but it quickly recovered. Few people had spending money for entertainment outside the home, and radio grew even more popular. Some of the darkest years the nation had ever known became "the golden age of radio."

CHAPTER

THE GOLDEN AGE
OF RADIO

On the evening of March 12, 1933, tens of millions of Americans gathered around their radio sets to listen to the new president, Franklin Delano Roosevelt. It was perhaps the worst year of the Great Depression: the nation's economy was in tatters, and despair blanketed the country. The president came on the radio, his voice smooth, calm, conversational. He summarized the actions he was taking to deal with the nation's crisis and invited his listeners to comment. He emphasized that effective government must be a cooperative effort of the people: "It is your problem no less than it is mine."

The response to the first of Roosevelt's many "fireside chats" was dramatic. What impressed people most was not what he'd said, but the personal, friendly tone he'd used. He'd given them a sense that government cared, that they were not alone. Many went to bed that night with the first stirrings of hope they had felt in many months.

Radio broadcasting was entering its time of greatest power as a political tool. In the years to come it would be used by many leaders who, like Roosevelt, sought to do good. Others would harness radio for evil purposes.

RADIO NEWS AND ENTERTAINMENT

People turned increasingly to radio for news in the turbulent 1930s. Listeners could hear accounts of fast-breaking stories on the radio hours before the next newspaper edition "hit the street." Improved equipment made it possible for mobile news-gathering teams to rush to the scene of a story for "on-the-scene" broadcasts.

New equipment also made it possible for radio to broadcast live conversations with news makers halfway around the world. NBC announcers in New York City spoke with Admiral Richard Byrd on his arrival in New Zealand from an expedition to Antarctica. Another New York announcer interviewed Marconi by radio as the great inventor sailed on his yacht off the coast of Italy.

Listeners tuned in to hear more than the news of the day. Radio comedies, plays, and variety shows brightened the evenings of the Depression. So powerful was radio's grip on the imagination of its listeners that one radio play nearly touched off a national panic. On October 30, 1938, CBS presented *The War of the Worlds*, a play about a Martian invasion of Earth. The play's news-broadcast style was so realistic that thousands fled their homes or hid in their basements. The CBS switchboards were overloaded with calls from terrified listeners. Only repeated announcements that it had been merely a play calmed the public.

BETTER EQUIPMENT

The radio stations of the 1930s were far more advanced than the early stations established in the wake of KDKA's success. In 1923, the world's most powerful station had a transmitting power of 500 watts. Ten years later 50,000-watt stations were commonplace, and some were seeking authorization to broadcast at 500,000 watts. Better equipment made broadcasting signals more stable, and listeners had to spend less time fiddling with the tuning control.

In the 1930s and 1940s, radio occupied a similar position in many homes that television does today.

Radio listening was no longer just a fireside activity. Millions of car radios were purchased in the early 1930s. Compact transmitters were soon on the market, too. Police and fire departments established two-way radio networks. "Radio dispatched" taxicabs and delivery vehicles became commonplace.

Stronger regulation was needed as the number and variety of radio stations grew. Some stations broadcast false advertising, dangerous medical advice, and racist propaganda. Many stations casually ignored frequency assignments and transmitter power limits. In 1934, Congress replaced the Federal Radio Commission with a stronger agency, the Federal Communications Commission (FCC).

FREQUENCY MODULATION (FM)

So much money had been invested to equip AM radio stations that the industry was slow to adopt a brilliant innovation. In 1933, Edwin Armstrong announced that he had perfected a different method of mixing audio signals with a carrier wave: frequency modulation (FM). Instead of modulating the amplitude of the carrier, he left the amplitude constant and modulated the frequency (Figure 11).

FM had a "cleaner" sound because it was less subject to interference. Static electricity in the atmosphere, certain kinds of motors, and sparks of any kind produced unwanted modulation of an AM signal's amplitude. The listener heard the interference as crackling or popping. In FM changes in the amplitude made no difference because the audio signal was encoded in small changes in the frequency of the broadcast signal.

RCA—an independent company after the breakup of the radio monopoly under government pressure—was interested in FM. With great hopes, Armstrong started experimental FM broadcasting from the top of the Empire State Building in New York City. He was soon told to remove his antennas. David Sarnoff, the president of RCA, had a different use for the world's

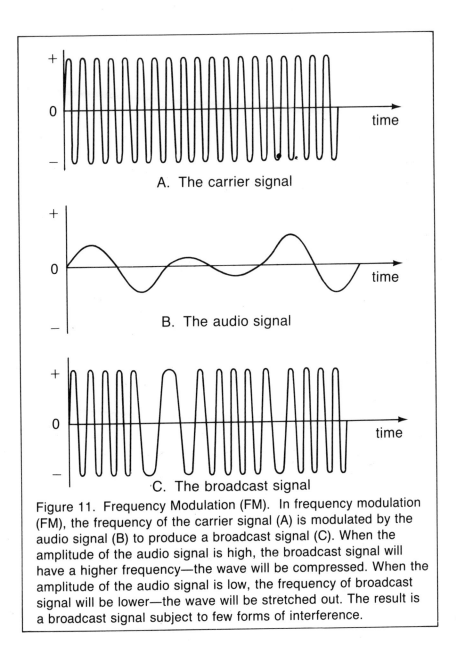

A. The carrier signal

B. The audio signal

C. The broadcast signal

Figure 11. Frequency Modulation (FM). In frequency modulation (FM), the frequency of the carrier signal (A) is modulated by the audio signal (B) to produce a broadcast signal (C). When the amplitude of the audio signal is high, the broadcast signal will have a higher frequency—the wave will be compressed. When the amplitude of the audio signal is low, the frequency of broadcast signal will be lower—the wave will be stretched out. The result is a broadcast signal subject to few forms of interference.

tallest building: the installation of an experimental television station. Armstrong began a long and frustrating search for acceptance of FM.

Even in its time of greatest popularity and power, radio was facing a new rival. For years, scientists and engineers had dreamed of transmitting moving pictures with electromagnetic waves. Sarnoff and Vladimir Zworykin, the head of the RCA research team, were determined to make these dreams a reality. By 1936 their antennas had replaced Armstrong's atop the Empire State Building, and field tests began.

The next few years saw the rapid development of television. Yet, technological progress was being overshadowed by other events in the world. Almost nightly, the radio news featured coverage of events in Europe. The German dictator Adolf Hitler and the Italian strongman Benito Mussolini were stoking the fires of racial hatred and ultranationalism. A new war threatened a world just beginning to emerge from the Great Depression.

THE DEATH OF MARCONI

In his native Italy, Guglielmo Marconi found the politics of the day both fascinating and distracting. Marconi had continued his work in radio through the years. Yet, his life was filled with other demands. The vast Marconi Company required his guidance. High society sought his attention. Mussolini asked him to perform diplomatic missions. (Always the patriot, Marconi readily agreed, but his enthusiasm for the strutting dictator soon faded.)

Marconi enjoyed the fame and honors heaped on him by an admiring world. Yet, as his health began to fail, he often longed for the earlier times when he had been able to pursue his inventions with a single-minded purpose. He died on July 20, 1937. That night many radio stations around the world ceased transmission for two minutes in honor of the father of radio. Then it was business as usual. Radio had become too important to humankind to pause longer.

TELEVISION AND FM BROADCASTING

In early 1938 Armstrong completed work on the world's first commercial FM station, W2XMN in Alpine, New Jersey. There was no sudden rush to change to FM, but soon a handful of stations were demonstrating that FM sound was superior to AM. Even more worrisome to the entrenched radio industry was the news from New York.

RCA began regular television broadcasting during the New York World's Fair in the summer of 1939. Thousands flocked to see demonstration models, and a few sets were put on sale for $625. The price was high—a new car could be bought for $900—the screen tiny, and reception poor. Still, 1939 might have been the dawn of the television age except for a great catastrophe. On September 1, 1939, Nazi Germany invaded Poland, starting World War II. The commercial development of both FM radio and television slowed to a near halt as factories turned to making the weapons of war.

DARK HOURS FOR DEMOCRACY

The Nazis and their Italian allies quickly conquered most of Europe. Across the narrow English Channel, Britain held out. In the gloomy days of 1940, the people of Britain and occupied Europe heard the gravelly voice of Prime Minister Winston Churchill snarling defiance: "We shall fight on the beaches . . . we shall fight in the fields and in the streets, we shall fight in the hills; we shall never surrender."

Radio broadcasting was one of the great weapons of the war. Churchill and the other Allied leaders used it to rally the people of the threatened democracies. News broadcasts into occupied Europe kept the hope of victory alive. Hitler and Mussolini responded with savage denunciations of the Allies.

Peace ended for America on December 7, 1941, when Japanese planes bombed the naval base at Pearl Harbor, Hawaii.

Within hours, radio had spread the news across the country. The next day an estimated 80 percent of the nation's homes tuned in to hear President Roosevelt call for a declaration of war. In days the United States was at war with Japan, Germany, and Italy.

The armies and navies of World War II fought with far better radios than the clumsy equipment of the previous world war. FM was particularly well suited for the portable and mobile voice radios needed in the field. Highly reliable wireless telegraphy was used over long distances. The radio industry worked round the clock producing rugged equipment for military use.

Around the globe, Allied soldiers and sailors tuned in to the Armed Forces Radio Service (AFRS) for news and entertainment. The first worldwide voice network, the AFRS had some 800 stations by May 1945, when Nazi Germany collapsed. Three months later, the AFRS broadcast news of the dropping of an atomic bomb on the Japanese city of Hiroshima. Japan surrendered on September 2.

CHAPTER

7

THE
TRANSISTOR
REVOLUTION

It was unimpressive to the eye: a half-inch metal cylinder with two wire leads. Yet, to the scientists of Bell Laboratories, their invention was a thing of extraordinary beauty. The date was June 30, 1948, and the world's most powerful private laboratory was giving the first public demonstration of a revolutionary device: the transistor.

The excitement of the Bell scientists was not shared by most of the reporters who attended the demonstration. The next day's *New York Times* devoted four paragraphs on its last page to the transistor. The article dryly described how Bell Labs claimed that the transistor could replace vacuum tube amplifiers and oscillators. The writer seemed to attach little importance to the fact that the transistor was smaller, simpler, and promised more durability than vacuum tubes. Like the other reporters, he had missed the significance of one of the major scientific developments of the century.

The invention of the transistor marked the beginning of a revolution in radio technology. In a few years, transistors and similar components would change the shape, reliability, and uses of radio equipment.

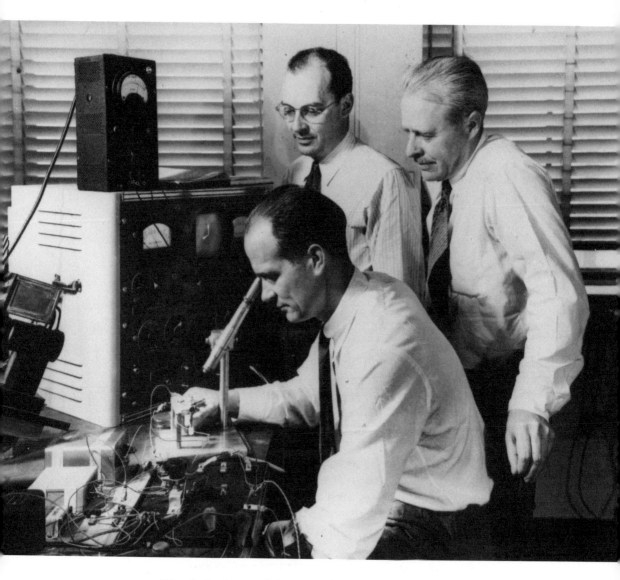

The inventors of the transistor: (from left to right)
William Shockley, John Bardeen, and Walter Brattain

THE DEVELOPMENT OF
THE TRANSISTOR

Lengthy investigation of a complex science called solid-state physics had led to the development of the transistor and similar solid-state components. The Bell Labs researchers produced pure crystals of materials called semiconductors. These materials shared some of the properties of both conductors (materials, such as copper, that allow the free flow of electricity) and insulators (materials, such as rubber, that block the flow of electricity).

Chemically treating semiconductor crystals produced two opposite types of semiconductors, P-type and N-type. (The P and N stood for positive and negative, respectively.) A slice of P-type fused to a slice of N-type produced a semiconductor diode that allowed the flow of electricity in only one direction. One type of material sandwiched between two slices of the other produced a semiconductor triode (a transistor) that could amplify a current.

Semiconductor components were marvelously simple and compact. They could be manufactured with ease, and their raw materials were cheap. (Silicon, a common semiconductor material, is only refined sand.) Unlike vacuum tubes, semiconductor— or solid-state—components did not have to be heated, so ran on a fraction of the power. Equipped with these new tools, engineers set about designing a vastly superior generation of radio equipment.

A BOOST FOR BROADCASTING

The development of solid-state radios gave the broadcasting industry a huge boost. Radio broadcasting had fallen on hard times since World War II. Television had gained popularity rapidly, replacing radio listening as America's favorite form of entertainment. Radio advertising revenues had plunged, and the radio networks had gone into decline.

By the mid-1950s the radio broadcasting industry was booming again. Portable, solid-state radios were selling at a phenomenal rate. While the television set sat stolidly in the family living room, a battery-powered "transistor" radio could be taken on picnics, to the beach, on boating or camping trips . . . virtually anywhere.

FM RADIO

The vast majority of radio stations were still AM. Since the introduction of FM broadcasting in the late 1930s, serious music listeners had championed its superior sound. However, the development of FM broadcasting was thwarted again and again. In 1945, the government moved the FM band to a higher frequency range, making all prewar FM receivers obsolete. Even worse, the higher frequencies reduced the range of FM signals. Many AM stations broadcast their programs on FM as well, but only a small number of listeners saw any point in buying FM sets to receive duplicate programs of short range.

Edwin Armstrong watched the squandering of FM's future with deepening frustration. He accused RCA of trying to destroy FM radio broadcasting. In 1948, he sued RCA for unauthorized use of his patents in the transmission of television sound. Legal proceedings dragged on for years. In 1954, depressed and in declining health, Edwin Armstrong—probably the greatest radio engineer America had ever produced—stepped from the window of his thirteenth-floor apartment. Armstrong's suicide was all the more tragic because his faith in FM would be justified in the coming years.

In the late 1950s, stereo records and home players started coming on the market. A stereo recording was made with two microphones located in different parts of a concert hall or recording studio. A stereo record preserved these separate inputs on two tracks for play through separate speakers. In the home, ste-

An early stereo system

An announcer in the control room at WNYC-FM in New York
City. The console can be used for nationwide call-in
shows and as an on-air studio. (Compare the setup here,
which is only a small part of the electronic equipment
at the station, with the KDKA setups shown in Chapter 5.)

reo gave the listener a far better sense of how the music had sounded when originally performed.

Soon consumers were calling for radio broadcasts of the quality provided by stereo records. The radio industry began to reexamine FM. Besides its near immunity to most forms of interference, FM used wider frequency channels than AM, reproducing the range of audio sounds from high to low with greater accuracy. Experimentation with FM stereo broadcasting was soon under way. The FCC licensed regular broadcasts in 1961.

THE STEREO SIGNAL

Stereo radio broadcasting is simple enough in concept. Half the broadcast signal is wasted in conventional broadcasting, since the audio is reproduced on the top and the bottom. If all radios were stereo sets, the two different audio channels could be encoded on opposite sides of the broadcast signal. However, early FM sets were nonstereo (mono) sets. A complex procedure called frequency-division multiplexing was designed so that both mono and stereo sets could get the best possible sound from a stereo broadcast (Figure 12).

The multiplexing of a stereo broadcast signal requires some complicated techniques, but in effect both sides of the broadcast signal carry both audio channels, although not in the same form. A mono receiver ignores the lower half of the signal and plays the audio channels on the top half through a single speaker. A stereo receiver subtracts one audio channel from the top half of the broadcast signal and the opposite audio channel from the bottom half, producing two different audio signals for play through two speakers.

MICROWAVE COMMUNICATIONS

The complicated engineering feat of producing stereo broadcasting mattered little to average listeners. Nor did most realize that

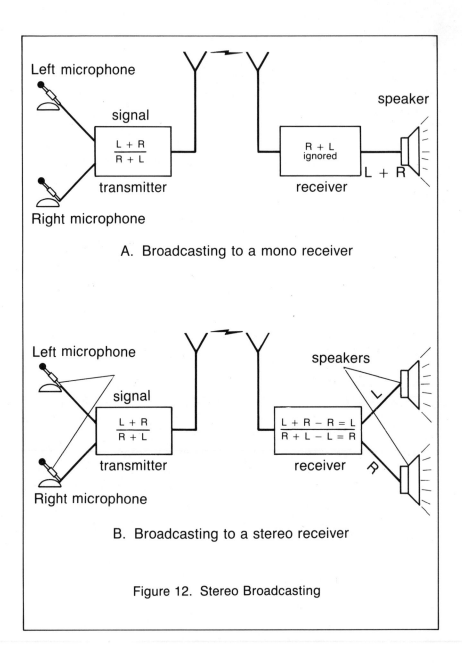

Left microphone

signal

speaker

$$\frac{L + R}{R + L}$$

R + L
ignored

L + R

transmitter

receiver

Right microphone

A. Broadcasting to a mono receiver

Left microphone

signal

speakers

$$\frac{L + R}{R + L}$$

$$\frac{L + R - R = L}{R + L - L = R}$$

L

transmitter

receiver

R

Right microphone

B. Broadcasting to a stereo receiver

Figure 12. Stereo Broadcasting

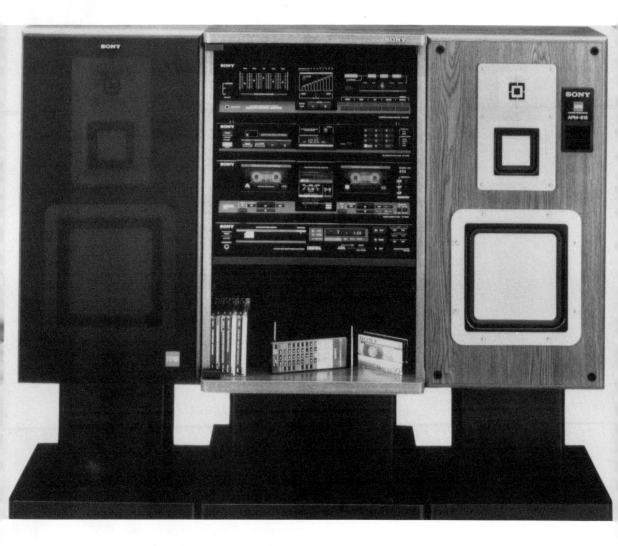

*Speakers aside, the equipment shown here—radio,
two cassette recorders, and specialized sound-controlling
hardware—occupies about the same amount of space
as the large radio shown in Chapter 6.*

advances in radio science were giving people better two-way communications. Long-distance telephone conversations were more and more often being sent through a highly efficient system combining both conventional wires and ultrahigh-frequency radio waves called microwaves.

Radio engineers had long appreciated the advantages of using radio waves in the microwave band of 1,000 to 300,000 million hertz, or Mhz. Microwaves were stable, predictable, and almost immune to static and most other forms of atmospheric disturbance. Late in life, Marconi had experimented with microwaves, and other engineers had developed their use in radar and short-range communications. However, microwaves were not considered of much use at distances of more than 30 miles (48 km) because they were not reflected by the ionosphere.

AT&T, the giant telephone company, had the funds and engineering know-how to overcome this disadvantage. Beginning in the late 1940s, it built a system of towers with directional antennas to relay microwave signals from point to point. In 1951, AT&T completed the first transcontinental microwave relay system. The system was efficient and continued to expand until microwave relay towers were a common sight by the early 1960s.

Yet, even AT&T could not afford to space relay ships at 30-mile intervals across the oceans. Intercontinental communications continued to depend on submarine cables and the over-crowded high-frequency band. AT&T turned its ambitions toward outer space.

On July 10, 1962, radio listeners heard news of a spectacular advance: the orbiting of Telstar, the world's first commercial communications satellite. Built by AT&T's Bell Labs and launched at the telephone company's expense, Telstar could receive, amplify, and retransmit radio signals across oceans and continents with amazing speed and efficiency. In a few short minutes, a Thor Delta rocket had hurled not only Telstar, but humankind into a new era of communications.

CHAPTER

8

RADIO IN
THE SPACE AGE

Today dozens of Telstar's descendents ring the earth, relaying radio messages, streams of computer data, television signals, and almost countless phone conversations. Communications satellites are masterworks of engineering, containing millions of solar-powered circuits. Every "comsat" launch is a delicate undertaking; the rocket booster must burn just long enough to propel the satellite into a precise orbit 22,300 miles (35,968 km) above the equator. There it can ride in a geosynchronous orbit, always above the same spot on the spinning world below (Figure 13). Alternately baked by the sun and frozen in the earth's shadow, the comsat will work round the clock year in and year out—another link in a communications network at the service of humankind.

The quarter-century since Telstar has seen remarkable progress in many areas of communications. It is no longer easy to talk about radio as an individual form of communications; the technologies of radio, computer, television, and telephone systems are too intertwined. As we survey today's communications systems, we can see the dazzling future of this expanding web of technologies.

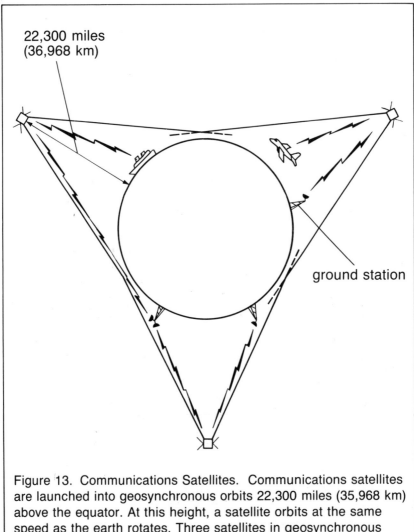

22,300 miles
(36,968 km)

ground station

Figure 13. Communications Satellites. Communications satellites are launched into geosynchronous orbits 22,300 miles (35,968 km) above the equator. At this height, a satellite orbits at the same speed as the earth rotates. Three satellites in geosynchronous orbit can provide communications coverage for the entire earth. However, many more have been launched to improve coverage and handle the millions of messages sent every day.

A composite photograph of Telstar

SPACE EXPLORATION

Increasingly, communications satellites share outer space with human beings. On earth, controllers use a network of microwave transmitters, relay stations, and directional antennas to send messages to space travelers. Return messages are sent by small, low-power transmitters on the spacecraft. The highly sensitive receivers and massive dish antennas at earth stations pick up the low-power transmissions. Voice transmissions from the travelers make up only a small portion of the messages received. Automatic systems aboard the spacecraft are constantly sending streams of data about the flight.

In the near future, there will be a permanent human presence in outer space. The workers aboard space stations will carry on even more advanced tasks and require even better communications systems. Their work may include the construction of spacecraft to carry human beings to the farthest reaches of the solar system. Unmanned space probes have already begun the process of unveiling the secrets of the outer planets. Their messages cross billions of miles to bring us scientific information and a vision of wonder beyond the imagination of previous generations.

MICROCHIPS

Our space program would have been virtually impossible without the development of tiny electronic devices called microchips. Microchips are made from small chips of semiconductor material chemically processed to contain hundreds of thousands of microscopic circuit components. The transistors invented in the 1940s now seem very bulky in comparison. Chips are more reliable, too. By one estimate, today's microchip circuits are 10,000 times more reliable than the transistors of the early 1960s.

The use of microchips has made communications equipment vastly more powerful, compact, and reliable. Microchips are so

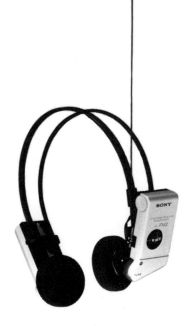

A headphone-radio combination

small and require so little electricity that tens of thousands of them can be packed into large pieces of equipment such as communications satellites. Built with individual transistors and diodes instead of microchips, Telstar could handle only 240 phone conversations at a time. Today's comsats can handle more than 36,000.

Advanced chip design and new materials will make the microchips of the next decade even more powerful. It is entirely possible that two-way, watch-size radios will be on the market in the next few years. With a new technology called cellular radio, these ultimately portable radios may work with the reliability of telephones.

CELLULAR RADIO

Today a number of large cities have cellular radio (also called cellular telephone) networks (Figure 14). At present, these networks are used mostly for car telephone service. A cellular radio network divides a city into blocks of six-sided cells. Each cell is assigned a group of frequencies. (Sometimes these frequencies are unused portions of FM broadcast channels.) Within a block, a frequency is never assigned twice. Frequencies will be duplicated in adjoining blocks, but since cellular radios have low transmitting power, there are few interference problems.

The driver of a car with a cellular radio places a call through a relay station to a control center at the telephone company. The control center completes the call through the regular telephone system. When the car crosses into another cell, a different relay station automatically takes over, and the radio is switched to a frequency assigned to that cell. The conversation of the parties "on the line" is uninterrupted.

When a car's cellular radio is not in use, it broadcasts its number with a low-powered radio signal. If someone in the city wants to contact the driver, the control center pages all cellular radio signals for the right number. The paging is done by direction-finding equipment at the relay stations.

COMPUTERS AND RADIO

A microchip that contains all the circuits for a simple computer is called a microprocessor. Microprocessors perform important functions in many of today's radios. Digital readouts, remote tuning, and programmed memories are but a few functions made possible by microprocessors.

A cellular radio

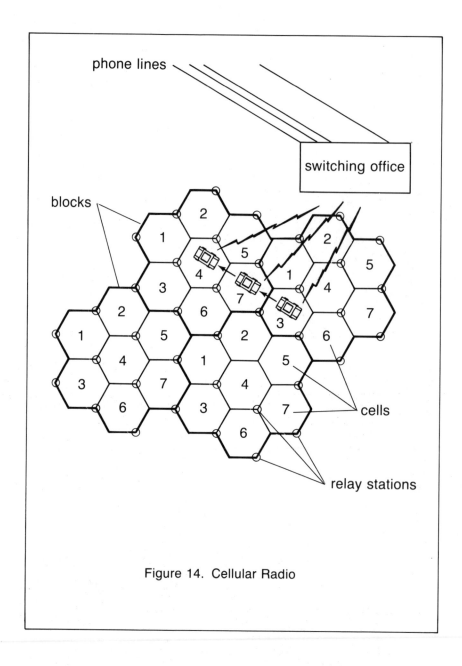

Figure 14. Cellular Radio

Microprocessors, like almost all computers, are digital devices. A digital computer recognizes only two states: on and off. We represent these states as 1's and 0's in a numbering system called binary. Letters, numbers, music, pictures, and many other forms of information can be represented as strings of 1's and 0's. The simplicity of binary makes transmission, reception, and duplication of digital information extremely reliable.

In our world more and more information is being processed in digital form. Government and private organizations have built huge storehouses of information called data bases. Computers exchange immense quantities of information over phone lines. In the next decade, it may become possible for users of hand-held computers to tap into data bases using a new technology called packet radio (Figure 15).

Packet radio uses a very reliable type of modulation called pulse code modulation (PCM) to send and receive digital information. In PCM a pulse of radio energy represents a 1, a pause, a 0. PCM information can be transmitted much faster than it can be processed by printers and similar equipment at the receiving station. To get the maximum use out of a frequency channel, a technique called time-division multiplexing (TDM) is employed. At the transmitting station, a computer "chops" messages for several receivers into small blocks. The transmitter then spends a fraction of a second sending each block to its intended receiver. About the time the first receiving station has processed its first block, the transmitter will send it a second, and so on down the line.

PACKET RADIO AT WORK

Packet radio could have many life-saving applications in the near future. For example, in the early 1990s a paramedic in Los Angeles arrives on the scene of an accident where a visiting motorist from Anchorage, Alaska, lies unconscious. The paramedic desperately needs to know if the motorist is allergic to any

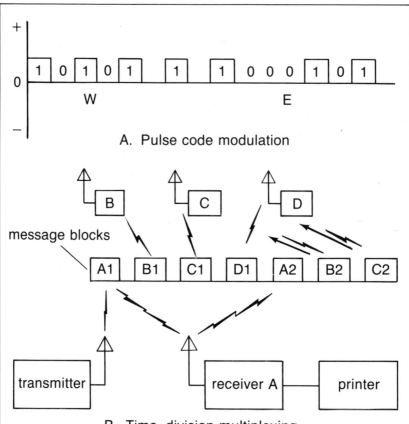

A. Pulse code modulation

message blocks

B. Time–division multiplexing

Figure 15. Packet Radio. Packet radio uses pulse code modulation (PCM) to send and receive digital information. Figure 15A shows a PCM signal for the series of 1's and 0's that represent the letters W and E in a common computer code. Time-division multiplexing (Figure 15B) makes it possible to send PCM messages to several receivers in a short time. While the printer at A is processing block A1, the transmitter sends blocks B1, C1, and D1 to other receivers. About the time the printer at A is done with block A1, the transmitter will send it block A2, and so on.

drugs. He types a request on the keyboard of his packet radio. The radio sends the message to the relay station at the LA hospital, which retransmits it to a communications satellite for further relay to the hospital in Anchorage. In seconds the computer at the hospital in Anchorage is sending the answer in the other direction. The paramedic receives the information he wants in time to give prompt emergency treatment.

Packet radio has many other potential uses. Tiny radio transmitters may be attached to burglar and fire alarms to send immediate warnings to police and fire departments. Radios attached to utility meters may report our monthly usage directly to the billing department. In cars, packet radios could identify ownership at toll booths, open garage doors, or broadcast traffic violations to the police. Small, almost indestructible monitors could be dropped into remote areas to send radio warnings of forest fires, earthquakes, severe storms, or volcanoes.

IMPROVED RADIO BROADCASTING

Today there are more than 8,000 radio stations in the United States and the old problems of station interference are all too common. Future generations of transmitters and receivers may work with pulse code modulation rather than AM or FM. PCM combined with time-division multiplexing could provide better reception, more services, and higher reliability.

Other avenues are also being explored to make radio broadcasting better. With another form of multiplexing, called frequency-division multiplexing, several channels of information can be encoded on a single broadcast signal. Some stereo stations now broadcast not only two channels of stereo, but one or more channels of information for such specialized uses as data transfer, cellular telephone, and background music for stores and offices.

The value of previously unused frequencies is also being studied. There is experimentation with millimeter waves of even

The new master control link and satellite distribution center at WNYC-AM and WNYC-FM in New York City

higher frequencies than microwaves. Extremely low frequencies are being used to send signals through earth and water. The navy is testing a system for sending messages to submarines from airplanes and satellites with lasers and light waves.

TOWARD THE YEAR 2000

Our modern world has an enormous appetite for communications. Never before have we had so much information or the need to send and receive it with greater speed and efficiency. We expect a great deal from our communications services. We want information and entertainment tailored to our individual needs and tastes. We want services that are cheap, reliable, and instantly available. The communications scientists and engineers working to improve and expand our communications systems follow in the footsteps of such courageous achievers as Tesla, Fessenden, De Forest, Armstrong, and Marconi.

Marconi's feat of spanning the Atlantic is dwarfed, but not diminished by our ability to communicate over the billions of miles to our farthest-flung space probes. On that dreary December afternoon in 1901, Guglielmo Marconi and his small band of assistants opened a new era for humankind. No one that day could have imagined the powerful and versatile communications systems of today. Nor can anyone today fully imagine the systems of the future. In all likelihood, Marconi's dreams and ours will be realized beyond anyone's expectations.

FURTHER READING

Buckwalter, Len. *Beginner's Guide to Ham Radio.* Garden City, New York: Dolphin/Doubleday, 1978.

Gilmore, Susan. *What Goes On at a Radio Station.* Minneapolis: Carolrhoda Books, 1984.

Gunston, David. *Marconi: Father of Radio.* New York: Crowell-Collier, 1965.

LeBlanc, Wayne, and Carter, Alden. *Modern Electronics.* New York: Franklin Watts, 1986.

Settel, Irving. *A Pictorial History of Radio.* New York: Grosset and Dunlap, 1967.

Storrs, Graham. *The Telecommunications Revolution.* New York: Franklin Watts, 1985.

Young, Frank. *Radio and Radar.* New York: Franklin Watts, 1984.

INDEX

THE AUTHOR

Alden R. Carter is a former Navy communications officer, radio announcer, and teacher. He now writes for young adults. His other books for Franklin Watts are *Supercomputers, Modern Electronics* (both with Wayne LeBlanc), and *Modern China*. His novels *Growing Season* (Coward-McCann, 1984) and *Wart, Son of Toad* (Putnam/Pacer Books, 1985) were selected as best books for young adults by the American Library Association. He lives with his wife, Carol, and their son, Brian Patrick, in Marshfield, Wisconsin.

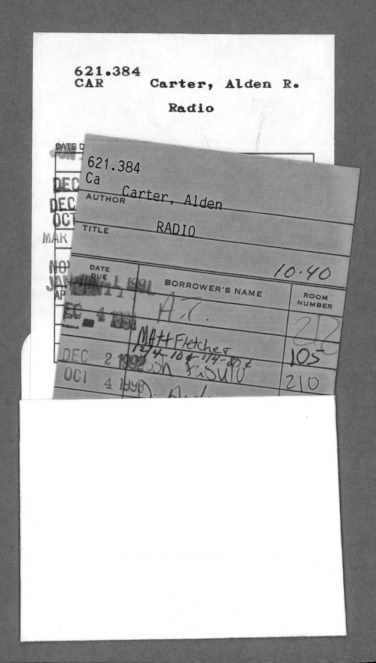